IDENTIFYING AS TRANSGENDER

SARA WOODS

ROSEN
PUBLISHING®

New York

Published in 2017 by The Rosen Publishing Group, Inc.
29 East 21st Street, New York, NY 10010

First Edition

Library of Congress Cataloging-in-Publication Data

Names: Woods, Sara, 1984– author.
Title: Identifying as transgender / Sara Woods.
Description: First Edition. | New York : Rosen Publishing, 2017. | Series:
  Transgender life | Audience: Grades 7–12. | Includes bibliographical
  references and index.
Identifiers: LCCN 2016018357 | ISBN 9781508173496 (library bound) | ISBN
  9781499464566 (pbk.) | ISBN 9781499464658 (6-pack)
Subjects: LCSH: Transgender people—Juvenile literature. |
  Transphobia—Juvenile literature. | Interpersonal relations—Juvenile
  literature. | Gender identity—Juvenile literature.
Classification: LCC HQ77.9 .W66 2017 | DDC 306.76/8—dc23
LC record available at https://lccn.loc.gov/2016018357

Manufactured in China

Some of the images in this book illustrate individuals who are models. The depictions do not imply actual situations or events.

CONTENTS

INTRODUCTION

"It's a boy!" "It's a girl!" From the moment we enter the world, the people and institutions in our lives—our parents, doctors, and governments—have already begun to relate to us through gender. Often even before we are born, doctors have already examined an ultrasound and assigned us to the categories of female or male. This assigned gender then appears on our birth certificates. From the beginning, it has far-reaching consequences in our lives—influencing the names we are given, the clothing we are dressed in, and the activities and skills we are encouraged to pursue. It affects how our parents, families, teachers, and friends all understand and interact with us.

Most people go on to navigate the world without ever questioning the *F* or *M* on their birth certificates, or the pronouns—she and her or he and him—used to describe their every action. They are able to move comfortably through their lives being seen as the gender assigned to them at birth. If their families call them girls as babies, they are able to live out their lives as girls and then women. If they are first called boys, they are able to live as boys and then men. These people are called cisgender—meaning that their sense of self does not conflict with their assigned gender.

Isaac Badillo, age sixteen, is a sophomore at Sterling High School in Sterling, Illinois. He is a trans man. While some transgender teens are trans men or trans women, others are nonbinary.

Many people, however, find that their assigned gender fails on a deep level to describe who they are. It does not allow them to live comfortably as themselves. These people realize that their gender is different from the one assigned to them at birth. Some come to understand that they are trans women: women who were assigned male at birth. Others may recognize themselves as trans men: men who were assigned female at birth. Many find that they identify with a combination of genders or with no gender at all and might use words like "agender," "genderqueer," "gender fluid," "bigender," "two-spirit," or "nonbinary" to describe themselves. No matter what their experience, anyone who does not identify exclusively with their assigned gender might consider themselves part of the broad category known as transgender.

Many transgender people decide to make personal changes in order to live more fully as themselves. They may change their names, use new pronouns, dress differently, adopt new mannerisms, or modify their bodies. Often, the process of making these changes is referred to as transitioning. Transitioning looks different for different people and does not necessarily have an endpoint. A person can spend their whole life exploring who they are and finding the most comfortable ways to inhabit their body.

This book provides an introduction to what it means to be transgender. You will learn about the amazing variety of gender identities and gender expressions that exist in our world, some of the challenges that trans people face, and some strategies that trans people have developed in order to live their lives as themselves. Welcome, my friends, to the gender galaxy.

CHAPTER 1

THE GENDER GALAXY: LIFE BEYOND THE BINARY

The genders assigned at birth do not accurately reflect everyone's identities. No matter what our bodies look like, or what gender our doctors and parents may believe us to have, our genders can only be defined by our own sense of who we are. Our gender identity, then, is the gender, or lack of gender, we each find best describes us.

Everyone, transgender and cisgender alike, has a gender identity. A cisgender person is a person whose gender identity is consistent with their assigned gender. A cis woman, for example, is a woman who was assigned female at birth. She was both assigned an *F* on her birth certificate and, when asked, will agree that her gender identity is female. Transgender people, on the other hand, have gender identities that do not match the genders assigned to them at birth. A trans woman is a woman who was assigned male at birth. She was assigned an *M* on her

Transgender women are women who were assigned male at birth. Some trans women come to identify as women after many years of life, while others identify as girls when they are toddlers.

birth certificate but comes to understand at some point in her life that her gender identity is actually female. It is important to note here that both cis women and trans women are women, and both have female gender identities. Similarly, trans men are men who were assigned female at birth. Both cis men and trans men are men, and both have male gender identities.

It is not always obvious what exactly a person's gender identity is, even to ourselves. We all come to know our gender identities at different times and in different ways. A man who is assigned female at birth, for example, may spend much of his life thinking of himself as female. The toys and clothes he is given when he is young are often those given to girls, and he will have a girl's name and be told by everyone around him that he is a girl, who will one day grow up to be a woman. Everyone he knows tells him he is a woman, and as he goes through puberty, he may find his body looking the way he is told women's bodies are supposed to look. Maybe he knows from the time he is very young—maybe as soon as he can talk—that he is a boy and wants to be treated as a boy. Or maybe it isn't until he is much, much older that he realizes he is not a woman. He might go his entire life, and then realize at age ninety that he is a man, despite the fact that his grandchildren have always called him Grandma.

There is no one path that all transgender people follow. Each person's experience is unique.

BEYOND THE BINARY

As you know, the most common gender identities in contemporary North America are male and female—or man and woman and boy and girl. In fact, these are the only two genders many people are aware of. Bathrooms, sports teams, and the boxes to check

Sports leagues and teams that are solely male or female often exclude trans people. Would a trans woman or nonbinary person feel safe and included on this women's soccer team?

on forms are all usually divided into these two categories. Boys' clothing and girls' clothing are sold on separate racks or even separate floors in a department store.

This system of dividing the world into two genders—male and female—is called the gender binary. For many of us, this system has come to seem natural. After all, most of us have lived with it every day of our lives beginning with the blues and pinks of infancy. In reality, there is nothing natural about it.

The system of assigning people male and female at birth may be the dominant system in contemporary United States and

Gender fluid people have genders that fluctuate. A gender fluid person might identify as a woman at times but at other times identify as a man, both a woman and a man, or neither.

Canada, but gender has looked very different in other places and at other times. In many cases, societies have included more than two and even more than three genders. Some contemporary examples of nonbinary genders include the *muxe* in Zapotec communities in southern Mexico, the *waria* in Indonesia, and the *mashoga* in Swahili-speaking areas of the Kenyan coast—each of these identities carries its own specific attributes and meanings.

Here in the United States, and Canada as well, many people fall outside of the binary. Some people are genderqueer or nonbinary—meaning that they may be neither male nor female or may exist between maleness and femaleness. Others are gender fluid, meaning that their gender fluctuates. Still others exist outside of gender altogether and use the term "agender" to describe themselves. In addition, many indigenous people are two-spirit, a term rooted in gender identities specific to some of the peoples indigenous to this continent.

GENDERS YOU MAY ENCOUNTER

There are many ways that people experience gender and many words people have used to describe their genders. Here are some common terms:

agender (*adj.*) Existing outside of gender altogether.

androgyne (*noun*) A person who is part male and part female, though not always equal parts each.

bigender (*adj.*) Identifying with two genders, usually male and female.

gender fluid (*adj.*) Having a gender that fluctuates.

gender nonconforming (*adj.*) Defying gender conventions. This umbrella term can include trans people—as well as drag queens, butch women, and many others.

genderqueer (*adj.*) Neither exclusively feminine nor exclusively masculine; having a gender identity that falls outside or in between the binary categories of male and female.

neutrois (*adj. or noun*) Neutral or in between genders. This term was created by combining the word "neutral" with the French word *trois*, meaning "three"—in this case, referring to a "third gender."

nonbinary (*adj.*) A general catch-all term for nonmale and nonfemale identities (including agender, androgyne, genderqueer, and many others). Also a gender identity in its own right, falling outside or in between the binary categories of male and female.

transfemme/transfeminine (*adj.*) A catch-all term referring to trans women and other trans people who were assigned male at

transmasc/transmasculine (*adj.*) A catch-all term referring to trans men and trans people who were assigned female at birth who lean masculine. Can also refer to a gender identity in its own right.

two-spirit (*adj.*) A term used by indigenous North Americans who fulfill one of many mixed gender roles rooted in the longtime gender systems of a variety of indigenous peoples. Unlike "transgender," this term can refer both to nonbinary gender identities and to queer or nonheterosexual identities, which may not be entirely separate.

WELCOME TO THE GENDER GALAXY

Because of this wide variety of genders, it is common for people to critique the gender binary by talking about gender as a spectrum, with male at one end and female at the other—and with all people existing somewhere between extreme maleness and extreme femaleness. But not everyone fits on a line between the categories of male and female or masculinity and femininity. Many people, such as agender people, exist outside of maleness and femaleness altogether. Others find that their gender identity changes over time.

In fact, there may be as many types of people, with as many relationships to gender, as there are people in the world. Instead of a spectrum, then, it may be helpful to imagine a whole gender galaxy—a three-dimensional space with an infinite number of moving gender possibilities. Male and female exist in this galaxy, but they are not centered within it. They exist alongside many other genders, each with their own particular ways of being: gender planets, gender stars, a gender black hole or two, gender asteroids, and giant clouds of gender space dust.

GENDER EXPRESSION AND GENDER NONCONFORMITY

Within the gender galaxy, there are as many different ways that people express their gender identities as there are gender identities themselves. Gender expression is the outward presentation of gender through clothing, hairstyle, and mannerisms. For men, women, and nonbinary people alike, these forms of expression vary quite a bit. There is no one way to look or act like a man, a woman, or a nonbinary person.

Think of the people in your life. Do know any girls or women who have short hair? Any boys or men who wear nail polish or jewelry? Girls who play hockey? Boys who dance ballet? There is as much variation among trans men and trans women as there is among cis men and cis women. Many trans women express their gender with mascara and high heels, but many also wear baggy pants and jerseys. A trans man might grow a beard and watch football, and he might like going out on the town in lipstick and glitter. Often, when people present in ways that deviate from the norms of binary gender, they may be referred to as gender nonconforming.

This woman is queer and gender nonconforming. Though she was assigned female at birth and identifies as a woman, her gender presentation falls outside of gendered expectations.

Nonbinary people also vary in the ways they choose to express their gender. A genderqueer person might mix masculine and feminine extremes—such as hiking boots and a slinky silk dress. Or they might avoid them, seeking a more neutral presentation. They also might tend to adopt clothes and hairstyles that are mostly associated with men or those that are mostly associated with women. As with all things gender, there is no wrong way to do it.

WHAT PRONOUNS DO YOU PREFER?

When we are talking about people, we often replace their names with pronouns. For example, Kanye West is a man and uses the

A NOTE ON SAFETY

People make choices about how they dress, talk, and move through the world for all sorts of reasons. Gender nonconformity is beautiful, but it does not always feel safe. People who believe strongly in the gender binary often target visibly trans and gender nonconforming people with harassment and violence. For this reason, many people, regardless of how they might personally prefer to dress, will decide to present themselves in ways that align with accepted binary gender norms. It is never wrong for a person to prioritize safety.

pronouns he, him, and his. If it is already clear whom we are talking about, we might refer to Kanye West without using his name and use only pronouns: "He is wearing his denim jacket today. His wife, Kim, gave it to him."

Pronouns are one form of gender expression. Generally, men—cis and trans alike—use he/him/his pronouns. Women most often use she/her/hers pronouns. Genderqueer, nonbinary, and agender people commonly use gender-neutral pronouns, such as they/them/theirs, ze/hir/hirs, or ze/zir/zirs. You may be unfamiliar with some of these pronouns, but don't worry. It's easy to learn how they work.

When you are introduced to somebody for the first time, it is a good idea to ask what pronouns the person uses. Letting a new friend know what pronouns you use is a good idea, too.

IDENTIFYING AS TRANSGENDER

When meeting someone new, it's always a good idea to ask what pronouns they prefer. Like clothing, a person's chosen pronouns might reflect their gender identity and presentation, but it is best never to assume. Some men and women prefer gender-neutral pronouns. Some genderqueer, agender, and gender fluid people may prefer to use she/her or he/him.

Here are some examples of possessive, subject, and object pronouns in action:

Her(s)/she/her: Her name is Irene. She loves dogs and dogs love her.

His/he/him: His name is Kirk. He is reading the book I gave him.

Their(s), they, them: Their name is Viridian. They love candy. We are bringing them some sour gummies.

Hir(s)/ze/hir: Hir name is Kael. Ze bikes for fun. Kael's girlfriend enjoys biking with hir.

Zir(s)/ze/zir: Zir name is Mae. Ze invited us to go camping with zir.

Which pronouns do you use?

CHAPTER 2

BODIES BEYOND THE BINARY

Human bodies are amazing. The chemical elements that are inside us—carbon, magnesium, calcium, and more—were originally forged in the deep, fiery bellies of faraway stars. Millennia later and light-years away, every one of us grew from just two cells into complex, unique creatures that never stop changing. Here we are, shoulders and belly buttons and kidneys, crawling and dancing, spitting and speaking across this planet Earth. But what do our star-born, cell-splitting bodies have to do with gender? Why are certain physical features commonly associated with the categories of male and female? How do transgender people relate to their bodies? What does it mean to be intersex?

CHROMOSOMES AND HORMONES

When doctors assign us genders at birth, they tend to make this assignment based on the appearance of our bodies. This practice depends on the popular concept that binary gender is built into our anatomy—that we each have an anatomical or biological sex.

Babies are often assigned genders before they are even born. Pink or blue clothes are one way that adults gender babies before they can articulate their gender for themselves.

In the popular imagination, this sex is defined by the appearance of our reproductive organs, our sex chromosomes, and the dominant types of hormones produced in our bodies.

None of these characteristics determine our gender identities. Our gender identities can only be determined by our own sense of who we are. In some bodies, these physical traits are paired in a way that is consistent with binary sex norms. Many people who have XX chromosomes, also have estrogen-dominant systems and reproductive organs typically labeled as female, for example. And many people who have XY chromosomes have testosterone-dominant systems and reproductive organs typically labeled as male.

Sometimes, however, bodies do not fit neatly into this binary. Just as there are more than two genders, there are also more than two types of bodies. For a long time, scientists believed that each person's DNA contained either XX or XY chromosomes, which determined a person's sex. They believed that XX made a person's body female, while XY made their body male. This is still a commonly held belief, taught in many schools. Some scientists, however, now object to the popular idea that XX and XY are the only types of sex chromosomes and that they correspond directly to male or female physical characteristics.

Most of us don't even know what our sex chromosomes look like because we go our whole lives without ever having them analyzed. Some women who were assigned female at birth actually happen to have XY chromosomes and never know it. Other people have XXY, XYY, XXYY, and other combinations of sex chromosomes that do not fit into a sex binary.

The idea that there are only two types of reproductive organs is also false. Reproductive organs, including genitalia, come in many forms. These frequently do not conform to male and female classifications. Our hormone levels, too, are incredibly variable. The levels of testosterone and estrogen in our bodies not only vary from person to person, regardless of gender, but also fluctuate throughout our lives. These hormones have a strong influence on our secondary sex characteristics, which are some of the most visible features associated with sex. These features—such as facial hair, Adam's apples, and breast size— can play a major role in how strangers see us, regardless of how we see ourselves. But they are much more varied than two categories alone can describe.

INTERSEX VARIATIONS

People whose combined physical traits diverge from binary sex categories are known as intersex. There are many ways to be intersex, many of which are not necessarily visible. An intersex person may have a different combination of hormones, reproductive organs, and sex chromosomes than a dyadic person. A dyadic person is a person who does not have intersex variations—meaning that their hormones, reproductive organs, and chromosomes fit into one of the two dominant sex categories.

Pidgeon Pagonis is an intersex activist and artist in Chicago, Illinois. Activists like Pagonis fight for their community's right to bodily autonomy and justice.

Most people are dyadic, but many people are intersex. The Intersex Society of North America estimates that approximately 1 in 100 people have bodies that deviate in some way from binary concepts of male and female. That's about 840,600 intersex people in New York City alone!

Like dyadic people, intersex people are usually assigned either male or female at birth. Because the concept of binary biological sex is so deeply ingrained in medical practice, many intersex people have been subject to nonconsensual treatments by doctors and surgeons, who try to make their bodies conform to one of the two binary sex categories. Often, they receive surgery as newborns to alter their genitals, for example. Many intersex people have fought to end this practice, demanding a right to make their own decisions about their bodies.

INTERSEX OR TRANSGENDER?

People often wrongly confuse the meanings of intersex and transgender. While some intersex people are transgender, many are not, identifying with the gender they were assigned at birth. Similarly, most transgender people are dyadic and do not have any intersex variations.

Intersex and transgender people do have much in common, however. Both intersex and transgender people are harmed by the myth of a biological sex binary. Both face discrimination and marginalization because their very existence defies this binary. And both have a right to make their own decisions about how to inhabit their bodies.

DYSPHORIA AND TRANS BODIES

In discussions about being transgender, you will often hear the word "dysphoria." Trans people often use this word to describe the anxiety and alienation they feel when their bodies or appearances conflict with the way they see themselves. For example, a transgender woman may feel dysphoria when she looks in the mirror and sees stubble on her face. Similarly, a trans man may feel dysphoria when he thinks about his breasts.

People also commonly experience dysphoria during their interactions with others because of the ways that others treat

Livvy James, age ten, and her mother give an interview about Livvy's experiences with gender dysphoria. Livvy is a transgender girl who was diagnosed with gender dysphoria in 2011.

them. They may feel dysphoria strongly, for example, when they are misgendered, or called by a gender other than their own. A clerk at the grocery store may say, "Have a good night, bro," and cause a whole eruption of difficult emotions in a trans woman's heart. This is one reason why it is best never to assume you know another person's gender, or with which pronouns they like to be addressed.

The painful experience of dysphoria has many sources and impacts many transgender people. But it is not universal. Many find that they are comfortable with their bodies as they are. This fact does not make them any less or more trans. The presence or absence of dysphoria is not a litmus test for a person's gender identity.

Those who do live with dysphoria may decide they want to make changes to their bodies in order to alleviate this feeling. They may choose to undergo hormone replacement therapy (HRT), for example. Both transgender people with dysphoria and those without it may seek out this treatment in order to better synchronize their bodies with their sense of who they are. HRT is a process that changes the balance of hormones in a person's body. It can help someone to shift their body from operating primarily with testosterone to operating primarily with estrogen. Similarly, it can help someone to shift their body from operating primarily with estrogen to operating primarily with testosterone.

Hormones influence many aspects of our bodies. People who undergo this therapy tend to see changes in their physical appearances, including their facial and body hair, and in the way that their fat is distributed. It can also have effects on the ways they experience emotions and intimacy. Trans women and other people who undergo estrogen HRT will notice that their hips, thighs, breasts, and butt will all begin to fill out more. Those who

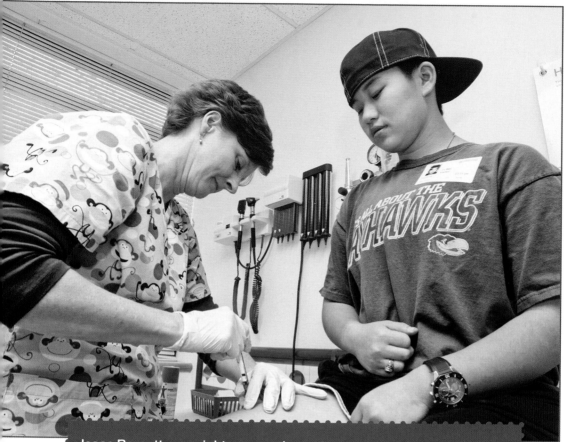

Isaac Barnett, age eighteen, receives a testosterone shot at Children's Mercy South in Overland Park, Kansas. Testosterone is a hormone that may be included as a part of hormone replacement therapy.

undergo testosterone HRT will notice that their voices get deeper and that they begin to build muscle more easily. They may also grow beards.

Young transgender people who are beginning to feel the effects of puberty may choose to receive a type of HRT called puberty blockers. Puberty blockers are medications that inhibit the effects of testosterone and estrogen, stopping or delaying a person's puberty. Young trans people can then take hormonal supplements in order to undergo the pubertal changes that feel best for them.

ACCESS TO CARE

Today, when a transgender person goes to the doctor seeking HRT or other trans-specific health care, they are likely to be diagnosed with gender dysphoria. In fact, this diagnosis is often required for a transgender person to gain access to treatment. While "dysphoria" is a term many transgender people use to describe a specific aspect of their experience, it is not something that all transgender people face. Nondysphoric trans people can be denied care because they do not fit a specific profile.

Gender dysphoria is not the first diagnosis to be used by medical institutions and insurance companies to deny or allow transgender patients access to care. As late as 1980, most trans people were diagnosed with "transvestitism" and refused medical care. In those days, a lucky few were diagnosed with "transsexualism" and considered for treatment. For a long time, in fact, doctors subjected transgender patients to strict scrutiny. Very few were able to access the medical care they needed. Trans people had few advocates among doctors and were considered to have a mental illness.

Thanks to the efforts of transgender activists and health care providers, however, accessing services is much easier for trans people now than it used to be. Many trans people are still forced to go through unnecessary mental health evaluations in order to receive treatments and services. But the criteria for these evaluations have become much more relaxed than they were twenty or forty years ago. A lot of progress has been made, but trans people today are still fighting for access to the medical care they need—and for the freedom to decide for themselves how to care for their bodies.

Hormone replacement therapy isn't right for every transgender person, but many people find it very helpful. The decision to seek out a treatment should always be up to the individual. If hormone replacement therapy sounds interesting to you, it might be worthwhile to seek out a trans-friendly doctor in your area.

In addition to HRT, there are other medical procedures that transgender people commonly choose to pursue. Some transgender people are uncomfortable with their chests or breasts. They may seek out top surgery, which refers to the removal or enlargement of breasts. Others don't like their genitals and choose to have them altered through bottom surgery. There are many different procedures a person seeking bottom surgery can choose from, depending on how exactly they want their body to change. Contrary to common misconceptions, not all trans people want bottom surgery or want the same kind of bottom surgery. The decision to receive or not receive any type of treatment is very personal.

Many trans people have dysphoria relating to their faces as well. Trans women and transfeminine people commonly undergo facial feminization surgery (FFS), which can subtly alter a person's facial features. They may also seek out professional facial hair removal, through the methods of electrolysis or laser hair removal. Because estrogen does not help to alter vocal chords, many transfeminine people also go through vocal training in order to change the sound of their voices. Testosterone, on the other hand, will often significantly affect both a person's voice and face shape—so transmasculine people are less likely to seek out these kinds of procedures.

CHAPTER 3

WHO WE ARE AND WHOM WE DATE: TRANSNESS, ORIENTATION, AND RELATIONSHIPS

Many people first hear about transgender people as a part of the LGBTQIA+ acronym. It stands for "lesbian, gay, bisexual, transgender, queer or questioning, intersex, and asexual." However, many people are confused about the meanings of these words. People also wonder why they are so often lumped together. You may have questions of your own. What is the relationship between gender identity and orientation? Whom do transgender people date? How do they describe their orientations?

WHOM WE DATE

For many people, gender identity and sexual orientation are entirely separate. Gender identity is about who we are, while sexual orientation is about whom we date. Just like cisgender

This happy heterosexual couple consists of a transgender man and a cisgender woman. Like cis people, trans people can be either gay or straight.

people, transgender people can be gay or straight. They can also be bisexual, pansexual, queer, asexual, graysexual, aromantic, or polyamorous. In fact, they can have any of the orientations that a cis person can have.

Often, trans people develop new understandings of their orientations after they come out as transgender. For example, a trans woman who primarily dated men before transitioning may have presented herself to the world as a gay man at that time in her life. If she continues to date men after coming out, she will likely call herself a straight woman, even if she is in the very same relationship she called a gay relationship in the past.

It is also not uncommon for transgender people to experience changes in whom they are attracted to. For example, a trans man may have been attracted to men before he came out. At some point during his transition, he might begin to date women instead and consider himself a straight man.

Some transgender people find that they prefer to date other transgender people in order to have partners who more closely understand their experiences. There are trans women who date trans women, trans women who date trans men, trans men who date trans men, nonbinary people who date nonbinary people, and many other forms that trans relationships may take!

When it comes to nonbinary people, the dominant terms that we have for sexuality tend not to make much sense. Who, for example, would a straight agender person date? Would a genderqueer person only be homosexual if they dated other genderqueer people? What if they dated a gender fluid person? As these questions show, many transgender people defy binary ideas of gay and straight as well as male and female. For this reason, trans people may use more general terms to talk about their preferences. They might say something like, "I

Jamie Eagle and Louis Davies are a married couple. They are both transgender. Both Jaime and Louis identified as a gender different from their assigned gender from an early age.

mostly date feminine people," or, "I'm attracted to all genders, especially androgynous people," or, "I am primarily interested in other transmascs."

SEXUAL ORIENTATION AND GENDER IDENTITY

It is common these days for many people in the United States and Canada to emphasize the distinctions between gender identity and sexual orientation. Not everyone who is transgender is queer in orientation. And not everyone who is queer in orientation is transgender or even gender nonconforming.

While this distinction is important to understanding many identities in contemporary North America, a complete separation between gender- and orientation-related identities is actually pretty unique. In many times and places, gender and sexuality have not been seen as such separate identity categories.

In fact, in many cultures, gender and sexuality–variance are seen as related aspects of a person's identity. For example, nineteenth-century German thinkers commonly wrote about sexual orientation as just one of many aspects of gender identity. In contemporary times, many indigenous North Americans are two-spirit, a term that can refer both to nonbinary gender identities and also to queer or nonheterosexual identities. This term is rooted in the various gender systems that existed among many different peoples prior to colonization and which are not accurately reflected by the Eurocentric concepts of "lesbian," "gay," "bisexual," and "transgender." Similarly, identities such as the *hijra* in South Asia and the *bâkla* in the Philippines do not reflect such a rigid separation of gender and sexuality.

ORIENTATIONS YOU MAY ENCOUNTER

Sexuality is more than just gay and straight. Here are some words that people use to describe their orientations.

allosexual (*adj.*) Describes a person who experiences sexual attraction. An antonym of asexual in the same way that heterosexual

of all genders.

queer (*adj.*) An umbrella term for any gender and sexual identities that are not heterosexual or cisgender. Often considered to be reclaimed, this term has been used as a slur and is sometimes still used in its pejorative sense. Also used to describe a political orientation of people seeking to break with dominant norms around gender and sexuality.

straight (*adj.*) A man who is attracted exclusively to women or a woman who is attracted exclusively to men. Heterosexual.

TRANS FAMILIES

Transgender people have many different kinds of families. They are sons and daughters, siblings and cousins, aunts and uncles, parents, partners, and friends. Like cis people, they may form a long-term partnership, raise a St. Bernard together, and grow old as a couple knitting on the porch. Or they may form close relationships with a number of people and coparent children as a group. Others may prefer to live alone and find connection elsewhere.

One common misconception is that transgender people can't have children. Many transgender people do! First of all, many trans people come out later in life, when they already have had children. It is also not uncommon for an egg-producing transgender person to go through pregnancy and have a child with a sperm-producing partner or a sperm donor—or vice versa. Those who are on HRT may decide to pause their hormone treatment in order to make

Thomas Beattie, a transgender man, relaxes at home with his wife, Nancy Beattie, and their three children. Thomas gave birth to all three children.

fertilization and pregnancy biologically possible. Trans people also sometimes decide to store their sperm or eggs before beginning HRT, through a process known as cryobanking, in order to have children later. Others choose to adopt. There are many ways for transgender people to be loving parents.

Not everyone's family is accepting when a family member comes out as transgender. Some transgender people remain close with the family they grew up with. Others may not be able to maintain this relationship. Their family may not be welcoming, and staying in contact with family members may not be safe. Often, trans people seek instead to form families with the partners and friends they love and trust. Groups of queer and trans friends frequently come to rely on each other, live together, and may even raise children together as a chosen family.

CHAPTER 4

GENDER HURTS: TRANSPHOBIA, CISSEXISM, AND TRANS RESISTANCE

Bathrooms, sports teams, baby colors. So much of our world is structured around a binary system of gender and sex. For transgender people, this system can be difficult, scary, and even life-threatening. A simple trip to the bathroom can be a nauseating prospect, as a trans woman weighs the stares and harassment she may receive in the women's room against the discomfort or violence she may face in the men's. Can she get in and out before someone spots her and gets upset? At school, a teacher might call for the gym class to split into boys' and girls' teams, leaving a nonbinary student with nowhere to go. A trans man goes in for a check-up with his gynecologist and finds himself sitting uncomfortably in the waiting room of the "women's health" department. This everyday enforcement of the gender binary places the assumptions of cisgender people

Members of GetEQUAL, an LGBTQIA+ organization, rally in support of the Employment Non-Discrimination Act (ENDA). ENDA would make it illegal for employers to discriminate against LGBTQ people.

over the needs of transgender people. It is called cissexism. It is a form of structural violence—meaning that it is harm that is built into our society as a whole, rather than perpetrated primarily by individuals.

In addition to this structural violence, transgender people are also frequently the targets of discrimination, harassment, and abuse. They may be turned down for jobs or apartments. They may find themselves singled out by authority figures like teachers or police. This kind of discrimination is often referred to as transphobia. Transphobia is bias against or hatred directed toward transgender and gender-nonconforming people. It is very prevalent in our society. Beyond unfair treatment, exclusion, and the denial of resources, transphobic harassment and violence also threaten the safety and the lives of transgender people. When transphobia and cissexism are combined with other forms of oppression—such as racism, ableism, or poverty—they can have especially grave consequences.

BEING TRANS AT SCHOOL

Schools can be particularly miserable places to be transgender or gender nonconforming. Trans and gender-nonconforming

Lila Perry *(center left)* and friends outside Hillsboro High School in St. Louis, Missouri. Students walked out of class to protest the school's policies, which excluded Lila from using the women's restrooms.

students regularly experience slurs, bullying, harassment, and assault by students and teachers alike. Many school administrations, too, enforce policies that intentionally or unintentionally exclude and punish gender-nonconforming and transgender students. They may enforce a gendered dress code, for example, and require students to dress according to their assigned genders. Or they may refuse to recognize a student's chosen name and pronouns. This can be incredibly difficult at school, where students are often called on publicly by name.

Schools also often deny transgender students access to gender-segregated extracurricular activities, such as sports teams, and other gender-segregated spaces, such as restrooms and locker rooms. Transgender students may even be punished for attempting to use the facilities or programs that feel best to them. For nonbinary students, there is often no available team or restroom that feels comfortable. This kind of exclusion can set trans students up for additional harassment.

If you or someone close to you is experiencing harassment, discrimination, or exclusion around gender identity or gender expression, you are not alone. There are many groups and organizations that help to support and protect transgender and gender-nonconforming students experiencing this kind of treatment. If you have experienced or observed transphobia or cissexism at your school—or if you think your school could improve the way it treats its gender-nonconforming and transgender students—you can take a look at the action kits provided online by Transgender Law Center and Lambda Legal. They include lots of ideas and resources for making change. The hardships are real, but we can work together to care for one another and build communities that are safe and nourishing for everyone.

WHAT ABOUT YOUR SCHOOL?

Here are some questions that may be helpful in thinking about how your school treats its gender-nonconforming and transgender students:

- Do teachers and administrators respect and honor students' gender identity and expression?
- Do school records and class rosters accurately reflect transgender students' gender identities and names?
- If there is a school dress code, does it respect gender identity?
- Are restroom and locker room facilities safe and accessible for transgender students? Are there any gender-neutral facilities?
- What about sports teams?
- Do health classes and sexual education classes provide information for transgender students?
- Has your school published guidelines or held assemblies or workshops to promote the respectful treatment of transgender students?
- Do transgender and gender-nonconforming students experience discrimination or harassment?
- Do students know what to do and whom to talk to if they're discriminated against, harassed, or threatened because of their gender identity or expression?
- Do counselors provide helpful resources and referrals?

BEING TRANS AT HOME

One of the most difficult things that young transgender people (and older ones, too!) face is the prospect of coming out to parents and family. While some trans people have supportive families who are affirming of their gender, some trans youth face harassment, punishment, rejection, or abuse from their family at home. Some are even kicked out or choose to leave home because of the hostility they face. For this reason, trans people who still live with their families may choose to wait until after

Ayden Prehara *(right)*, a sixteen-year-old trans man, talks to his parents, Todd *(left)* and Chris *(center)*, in his bedroom in Fitchburg, Wisconsin. Ayden transitioned when he was fourteen.

they have moved out to come out to their families. They may choose to disclose their trans status first to friends or to adults they trust. They also may choose to come out, even in the face of possible rejection. This is an incredibly difficult decision. There is no right or wrong answer. What is right for you may not be right for another person. The important thing to remember is that there is nothing wrong with being transgender or with thinking that you might be. Any punishment or negativity you receive from your family is not your fault.

ONE OF MANY STRUGGLES

All transgender people are vulnerable to transphobia and cissexism. But there are groups of trans people who experience additional marginalization and mistreatment. Many transgender people face forms of oppression that have to do with other aspects of their identities. Like cisgender women, trans women and transfeminine people face a great deal of misogyny that trans men and masculine trans people may not face. This is called transmisogyny, and it can be the source of street harassment, sexual assault, and objectification. It is the reason that you may have noticed more negative attention and mean jokes in TV and movies about trans women than about trans men or nonbinary people.

Similarly, ableism combines with cissexism or transphobia to make life especially difficult for trans people who are also disabled. Ableism refers to the oppression of disabled people. This includes both structural violence, like exclusion from spaces and resources, and also discrimination and abuse. Many cities and towns, for instance, are not set up to provide adequate support and transportation to people with blindness or mobility issues. For this reason, a disabled trans person might have a much harder time getting to the doctor to get hormone treatments or to the courthouse to change identity documents. Disabled trans people, including those with invisible disabilities like chronic illness and mental health issues, may also face exclusion from queer and trans social scenes, organizations, and events that fail to make their spaces accessible or provide adequate resources.

Racism is another form of oppression that frequently combines with transphobia and cissexism to harm trans people of color in particularly serious ways. Black trans people—and

Marchers at the Gay Pride Parade in Rio de Janeiro in 2015. Pride is celebrated around the world on the anniversary of the New York City Stonewall Riots.

especially black trans women—commonly face elevated levels of harassment and violence from strangers, including police. In fact, black trans women are murdered at a rate higher than that of almost any other demographic in the United States. According to an article by journalist Diana Tourjee on the Vice website, there were twenty-three recorded murders of trans women in 2015, twenty of whom were black. Black people are also disproportionately targeted by the US justice and prison systems. This can have significant consequences for trans people, who are often placed in prisons according to their assigned gender rather than their gender identities. They are often mistreated by prison authorities and other inmates and denied access to hormone treatment and other medical care. Others are often held in isolation, a cruel and inhumane treatment in its own right.

Other trans people of color, including immigrants, also experience the combined effects of racism and transphobia. Undocumented transgender people—those who have not been granted legal immigration status in the country in which they currently live—face unique and unjust treatment. They are often unable to access health insurance or other services necessary to transition. They may also come up against significant barriers to obtaining documentation that matches their gender identities. Approaching a courthouse may feel unsafe, as they live with the constant threat of detention and deportation. Like prisoners in the US prison system, those who are detained are often placed in detention centers according to their assigned gender.

TRANS RESISTANCE

Perhaps because these groups of trans people have been the most marginalized and under attack, many of them have also been among the first to fight back on behalf of LGBTQ people everywhere. In fact, it was largely gay and transgender sex workers—most of whom were black and Latinx—who famously stood up to abusive police officers in the 1969 Stonewall Riots, an event often credited as the start of the gay rights movement. The Stonewall Riots were just one of many acts of resistance led largely by transgender women of color. During the civil rights, black power, American Indian, and Chicano movements, queer and transgender people of color began to stand up for their rights in many of the same ways that their cis counterparts were.

Nisha Ayub is a transgender rights activist in Malaysia. She runs SEED Foundation, a community-based organization in the country's capital, Kuala Lumpur.

As more normative white lesbian and gay people have increasingly integrated into mainstream society, often excluding transgender queer people of color, their history has frequently been erased. But transgender people have never stopped fighting. There is a long, strong history of trans resistance. Today, queer and transgender black women play a major role in the Black Lives Matter movement, which works against racist police violence and for the well-being of all black people. In June 2015, undocumented Latinx trans woman Jennicet Gutiérrez interrupted President Barack Obama's speech during a Pride celebration—calling attention to the horrific experiences of transgender women in immigrant detention centers and demanding their release.

As transgender people and their struggle for justice begins to receive more and more media attention, many trans people are working to see that the mistakes made by exclusionary white gay rights activists are not repeated. Their organizing focuses on the needs of the most vulnerable transgender people—sex workers, trans women of color, those who are disabled, those who are poor, those who are undocumented, and those who are incarcerated—as a first priority.

CHAPTER 5

FINDING LIFE IN THE GENDER GALAXY: TRANS FRIENDSHIP AND COMMUNITY

Transgender people face very real discrimination, harassment, and violence from the world around them. The truth is, coming out and transitioning can be a very scary prospect. A lot of times, it can feel completely overwhelming. This is something that every transgender person experiences, and that means that no trans person has to be alone through this struggle. There are a variety of ways that transgender people can and do find support, community, friendship, and family.

ORGANIZATIONS

Many larger towns and cities now have local LGBTQIA+ centers that host workshops, support groups, after-school programs, and events. These organizations often help transgender people

TORONTO PFLAG

Toronto PFLAG provides support for family and friends of LGBTQIA+ people in the area. It is one of many PFLAG chapters across North America.

connect with other queer and trans people, information, and resources. They are often able to provide location-specific information, such as the names of local trans-friendly doctors and therapists. The organizations may also be able to help with other trans-specific needs, such as the process of changing one's legal name and gender.

In addition to local community centers, there are national organizations that provide support for transgender people who need legal aid, help with housing, medical services, or support during a crisis. Many of these organizations also do work to advocate for transgender rights.

Suicide is probably the biggest issue facing the transgender community right now. All of the alienation, hate, harm, and unwelcomeness that is inflicted upon us every day might not leave physical scars, but it can lead us to create them ourselves. Suicide is the primary way transphobia takes lives. I, the author of this book, have struggled with it, and according to the National Transgender Discrimination Survey, almost half of my trans and gender–nonconforming siblings have attempted suicide at some point in their lives. I have seen strong trans people I love and respect lost to suicide. I am often scared, thinking about which of my friends and acquaintances will be lost next. The world is a very difficult place to be for a transgender person, and the temptation to give up can be strong.

If you are trans, or think you might be, and begin to feel the urge to hurt yourself, please reach out to someone you trust. If you don't know whom that might be, or if they aren't available, you can call the Trans Lifeline at (877) 565-8860 for US callers or (877) 330-6366 if you live in Canada. It might be useful to store the number in your cell phone or write it down and keep it with you. We all end up in dark places, but there is light for us. There is life for us. The world is more beautiful with trans people in it, and every day I am thankful for the wonderful transgender community I am part of. I am thankful for all of the beautiful, insightful trans people I look up to and admire, who have done so much to care for those around them. Since coming out and transitioning, I have found a world of other trans people who fiercely care for each other. I want you to have this, too. Keep your head up, and keep moving.

CONNECTING WITH OTHERS

Being a transgender person can be incredibly lonely when there are no other trans people around. Because of this, it can be very important to make connections with other trans people. Luckily, depending on where you live, there are a number of ways a person might go about meeting other transgender people. For example, if you are in a medium-to-large city, you might search online for local trans meetups. A number of cities hold regular Trans Lady Picnics or other similar kinds of social mixers. Many cities also

Social media sites such as Facebook, Tumblr, and Twitter are popular places for trans people to meet each other, share their stories, and build community.

hold transgender-focused poetry readings or showcases of local trans musicians. Places like this can be a great way to meet other trans people.

If you aren't in a big city, or if you are nervous about meeting other trans people in person, social media can be a great place to connect and network with other transgender people. There are hundreds of Facebook groups that exist for the purpose of connecting trans people with each other. Many focus on specific age groups, locations, identities, or interests. Tumblr and Twitter also have large trans communities and can be places to meet others.

ANRY FUENTES: TRANS CHEERLEADER

At Denair High School, in Denair, California, Anry Fuentes became the first trans girl on her school's cheerleading squad. Anry had come out as gay in her freshman year, but told reporters from *People* magazine that she later realized she "didn't even know what gay was." After doing some research, she realized that she was transgender. She broke the news to the rest of the cheer squad and was happy to find that they were all supportive of her.

Unfortunately, her mother was less so. After Anry came out, her mother threatened to throw away all of her things if Anry presented as feminine. Feeling she wasn't welcome at home, Anry decided to stay with a friend from the cheerleading squad instead. After being out at school and in cheerleading for a while, she was able to patch things up with her mom and eventually move back home. "I'm kind of glad that [my story is] getting out, so it can help others who are struggling," Anry said in the interview. "It makes me feel good, because I see that I'm helping."

LIFE AMONG THE STARS

The gender galaxy is wide and vast, and our journeys through it are all different. No one takes the same route or path, but it can help us to see where others have been. The important things to remember are that you are not alone and there are many others who can help you along the way. Though it has its difficulties, being transgender is amazing. Coming out and transitioning is a process of discovering yourself in new ways every day. Being transgender means finding new ways to live and be happy that you never could have thought were possible before. It means finding others who have had their own discoveries and connecting and sharing them with each other. No matter what you look like or feel like, no matter what you have been through, there is life for you among the stars.

GLOSSARY

ABLEISM Discrimination against people who are disabled.

AGENDER Existing outside of gender altogether.

ASSIGNED FEMALE AT BIRTH (AFAB)/ASSIGNED MALE AT BIRTH (AMAB) Having been assigned male or female by a doctor at birth (or in the womb before birth via ultrasound). This assignment does not determine a person's gender.

CISGENDER Referring to a person whose gender identity matches the gender they were assigned at birth.

CISNORMATIVITY When a person, institution, or society operates under the assumption that all people are cisgender, casually erasing or denying the existence of transgender people.

DYADIC Referring to a person who does not have intersex variations—meaning that their hormones, genitals, and chromosomes fit into one of the two dominant sex categories.

GENDER DYSPHORIA A medical term used to describe the distress, anxiety, or depression that may be caused when a transgender person's body or appearance conflicts with the way they see themself.

GENDER EXPRESSION The outward expression of gender through behavior, clothing, hairstyle, voice, or body characteristics.

GENDER FLUID Having a gender that fluctuates.

GENDER IDENTITY The gender a person sees themself as. It is completely independent of any aspect of that person's anatomy, gender expression, personality, or sexual orientation.

GENDER NONCONFORMING Defying gender conventions. This umbrella term can include trans people as well as drag queens, butch women, and many others.

GENDERQUEER Neither exclusively feminine nor exclusively masculine. Having a gender identity that falls outside or in between the binary categories of male and female.

HORMONE REPLACEMENT THERAPY (HRT) A process that changes the balance of hormones in a person's body.

INTERSEX Referring to a person whose chromosomes, genitalia, or hormone levels differ from rigid binary sex norms.

LATINX A gender-neutral term that encompasses all people of Latin American descent.

NONBINARY A catch-all term for nonmale and nonfemale identities (including agender, androgyne, genderqueer, and many others). Also a gender identity in its own right, one falling outside or in between the binary categories of male and female.

TRANS MAN A man who was assigned female at birth.

TRANSMISOGYNY Discrimination that specifically targets trans women and transfeminine AMAB people.

TRANSPHOBIA Discrimination against transgender people.

TRANS WOMAN A woman who was assigned male at birth.

FOR MORE INFORMATION

Black Trans Advocacy
3530 Forest Lane, Suite 38
Dallas, TX 75234
(855) 255-8636
Website: https://www.blacktrans.org
This organization is dedicated to serving black transgender and
gender-nonconforming people, who are one of society's most
discriminated-against groups. It has several outreach divisions,
including ones focused on identity development, economic
development, and legal and political issues.

National Center for Transgender Equality
1400 16th Street NW, Suite 510
Washington, DC 20036
(202) 642-4542
Website: http://www.transequality.org
Founded by transgender activists in 2003, the NCTE advocates
for the needs and rights of transgender people across the
United States. The group has a Transgender Legal Services
Network and its website has several suggestions for how
supporters can take action.

Rainbow Health Ontario
Sherbourne Health Centre
333 Sherbourne Street
Toronto, ON M5A 2S5
Canada
(416) 324-4100

Website: http://www.rainbowhealthontario.ca

Dedicated to extending health services to Ontario's LGBTQ community, Rainbow Health Ontario hosts events, offers access to a database of resources across the province, and promotes research into the health of LGBTQ people.

Sylvia Rivera Law Project
147 W 24th Street, 5th Floor
New York, NY 10011
(212) 337-8550
Website: http://srlp.org

This organization was founded to protect the rights of transgender individuals. Its mission states that "all people are free to self-determine their gender identity and expression, regardless of income or race, and without facing harassment, discrimination, or violence."

Transgender Law Center
1629 Telegraph Avenue, Suite 400
Oakland, CA 94612
(415) 865-0176
Website: http://transgenderlawcenter.org

People looking for legal information relating to trans issues can turn to the Transgender Law Center for help. The center's website offers easy access to legal information, as well as resources for dealing with issues such as housing, health, family law, and immigration.

TransLatin@ Coalition
1730 W Olympic Boulevard, Suite 300

Los Angeles, CA 90015

Website: http://www.translatinacoalition.org

As the group's website expresses, the TransLatin@ Coalition aims to "promote the empowerment of Trans leaders" and address the needs of members of the trans community of Latin American descent.

Trans Youth Equality Foundation

PO Box 7441

Portland, ME 04112

(207) 478-4087

Website: http://www.transyouthequality.org

Founded by the mother of a transgender child, the Trans Youth Equality Foundation aims to support young people who are transgender. The foundation holds youth retreats, hosts an educational podcast, and provides training for teachers and medical professionals.

WEBSITES

Because of the changing nature of internet links, Rosen Publishing has developed an online list of websites related to the subject of this book. This site is updated regularly. Please use this link to access the list:

http://www.rosenlinks.com/TL/ident

FOR FURTHER READING

Binaohan, B. *Decolonizing Trans/Gender 101.* Toronto, ON: Biyuti Publishing, 2014.

Bornstein, Kate. *My New Gender Workbook.* New York, NY: Routledge, 2013.

Coyote, Ivan, and Rae Spoon. *Gender Failure.* Vancouver, BC: Arsenal Pulp Press, 2014.

Edidi, Dane Figueroa. *Yemaya's Daughters.* Lulu.com Independent Publishing Platform, 2014.

Erickson-Schroth, Laura. *Trans Bodies, Trans Selves: A Resource for the Transgender Community.* New York, NY: Oxford University Press, 2014.

Gino, Alex. *George.* New York, NY: Scholastic Press, 2015.

King, Nia. *Queer and Trans Artists of Color: Stories of Some of Our Lives.* Createspace Independent Publishing Platform, 2014.

Kuklin, Susan. *Beyond Magenta: Transgender Teens Speak Out.* Somerville, MA: Candlewick Press, 2014.

Lam, Laura. *Pantomime.* Long Island City, NY: Strange Chemistry, 2013.

Lowry, Sassafras. *Roving Pack.* Brooklyn, NY: PoMo Freakshow Press, 2012.

Maroon, Everett. *The Unintentional Time Traveler.* Seattle, WA: Booktrope Editions, 2014.

Merbruja, Luna. *Trauma Queen.* Toronto, ON: Biyuti Publishing, 2013.

Mock, Janet. *Redefining Realness.* New York, NY: Atria Books, 2014.

Plett, Casey. *A Safe Girl to Love.* New York, NY: Topside Press, 2014.

Russo, Meredith. *If I Was Your Girl.* New York, NY: Flatiron Books, 2016.

Sonnie, Amy. *Revolutionary Voices: A Multicultural Queer Youth Anthology*. Los Angeles, CA: Alyson Books, 2000.

Stanley, Eric A., and Nat Smith. *Captive Genders: Trans Embodiment and the Prison Industrial Complex*. Oakland, CA: AK Press, 2011.

Stryker, Susan. *Transgender History.* Berkeley, CA: Seal Press, 2008.

BIBLIOGRAPHY

Asher. "Not Your Mom's Trans 101." *Tranarchism*, November 26, 2010. http://www.tranarchism.com/2010/11/26/not-your -moms-trans-101.

Binaohan, B. *Decolonizing Trans/Gender 101*. Toronto, ON: Biyuti Publishing, 2014.

Graffam, Catherine. "The Rift Between Us—Intersex and Trans Discourse." Medium, November 17, 2015. https://medium .com/gender-2-0/the-rift-between-us-intersex-and-trans -discourse-62dee7f7a73#.olw69hzdh.

Haas, Ann P., Ph.D., et al. "Suicide Attempts Among Transgender and Gender Non-Conforming Adults: Findings of the National Transgender Discrimination Survey." American Foundation for Suicide Prevention. Williams Institute, UCLA School of Law, January 2014. http://williamsinstitute.law.ucla.edu/wp -content/uploads/AFSP-Williams-Suicide-Report-Final.pdf.

Intersex Society of North America. "How Common Is Intersex?" Retrieved April 8, 2016. http://www.isna.org/faq/frequency.

Laqueur, Thomas. *Making Sex: The Body and Gender from the Greeks to Freud.* Cambridge, MA: Harvard University Press, 1990.

Marksamer, Jody, and Dylan Vade. "Trans 101." Sylvia Rivera Law Project. Retrieved April 8, 2016. http://srlp.org/resources/ trans-101.

McDonough, Katie. "CeCe McDonald on Her Time in Prison." Salon. January 19, 2014. http://www.salon.com/2014/01/19/ cece_mcdonald_on_her_time_in_prison_i_felt_like_they _wanted_me_to_hate_myself_as_a_trans_woman.

NativeOUT. "Two Spirit 101." April 8, 2016. http://nativeout.com/twospirit-rc/two-spirit-101.

Olya, Gabrielle. "Anry Fuentes Is the First Transgender Student on Her High School's Cheerleading Squad." *People*, November 7, 2015. http://www.people.com/article/anry-fuentes-first-transgender-cheerleader-high-school-team.

Richardson, Sarah S. *Sex Itself: The Search for Male and Female in the Human Genome.* Chicago; London: University of Chicago Press, 2013.

Robertson, Will. "Another Sex/Gender Controversy." *Skepchick*, October 23, 2013. http://skepchick.org/2013/10/44379.

Selva, Karen. "Puberty Blockers and Puberty Inhibitors." Trans Active Gender Center, April 8, 2016. https://www.transactiveonline.org/resources/youth/puberty-blockers.php.

Serano, Julia. *Whipping Girl: A Transsexual Woman on Sexism and the Scapegoating of Femininity.* Berkeley, CA: Seal Press, 2007.

Steadman, Ian. "Sex Isn't Chromosomes: The Story of a Century of Misconceptions about X & Y." *New Statesman*, February 23, 2015. http://www.newstatesman.com/future-proof/2015/02/sex-isn-t-chromosomes-story-century-misconceptions-about-x-y.

Stryker, Susan. *Transgender History*. Berkeley, CA: Seal Press, 2008.

Support Cece McDonald! WordPress. Retrieved April 8, 2016. https://supportcece.wordpress.com.

1NDEX

A

ableism, 38, 42–43
adoption, 35
agender, 5, 11, 12, 13, 17, 18, 31
allosexual, 33
androgyne, 12
androgynous, 32
aromantic, 30, 33
asexual, 29, 30, 33

B

bathrooms, access to, 9, 36, 39, 40
bigender, 5, 12
birth certificates, 4, 7, 9
bisexual, 29, 30, 32, 33
Black Lives Matter, 46
bottom surgery, 28
bullying, 39
butch women, 12

C

care, access to, 27, 44, 48
cissexism, 37, 38, 39, 42, 43
coming out, 30, 34, 41–42, 47, 49, 51, 52
cryobanking, 35

D

dating, 29–32
demisexual, 33
drag queens, 12
dress codes, 39, 40
dyadic, 22–23
dysphoria, 24–28

E

electrolysis, 28
estrogen, 20, 21, 25, 26, 28

F

Facebook groups, 51
facial feminization surgery (FFS), 28
Fuentes, Anry, 51

G

gay, 29, 30, 31, 32, 33, 45, 46, 51
gender fluid, 5, 11, 12, 18, 31
gender identity vs. sexual orientation, 29, 32–34
gender-neutral pronouns, 17, 18
genderqueer, 5, 11, 12, 16, 17, 18, 31
grayromantic, 33
graysexual, 30, 33
Gutiérrez, Jennicet, 46

H

hair removal, 28
hormone replacement therapy (HRT), 25–28, 34–35

I

intersex, 19, 21–23, 29
Intersex Society of North America, 23

L

Lambda Legal, 39
Latinx, 45, 46

ABOUT THE AUTHOR

Sara Woods is a writer living in Oregon. She is the author of three books of creative writing for adults, most recently *Careful Mountain* (available from CCM Press). When she isn't writing, she likes making art and spending time with any dogs that might be available.

She was born in southern Indiana and has a master's degree in library science from Indiana University. She is a genderqueer trans woman and is married to a wonderful person named Irene, who likes dogs as much as she does.

PHOTO CREDITS

Cover RoBeDeRo/E+/Getty Images; pp. 5, 22, 38, 41 © AP Images; p. 8 Leland Bobbe/The Image Bank/Getty Images; p. 10 Thomas Barwick/Iconica/Getty Images; p. 11 apomares/E+/Getty Images; p. 15 Patryce Bak/The Image Bank/Getty Images; p. 17 Westend61/Getty Images; p. 20 copyright by Elena Litsova Photography/Moment/Getty Images; p. 24 Steve Meddle/Rex Features/AP Images; p. 26 Kansas City Star/Tribune News Service/Getty Images; p. 30 Patryce Bak/Taxi/Getty Images; p. 31 Steve Meddle/Rex Features/AP Images; p. 35 Barcroft Media/Getty Images; p. 37 Alex Wong/Getty Images; p. 43 Mario Tama/Getty Images; p. 45 Manan Vatsyayana/AFP/Getty Images; p. 48 Hand-out/PFLAG Toronto/News.com; p. 50 Zave Smith/Image Source/Getty Images; cover and interior pages background graphic Shutterstock.com.

Designer: Nicole Russo; Editor: Amelie von Zumbusch; Photo Researcher: Nicole Baker